KYOZON

Taichi Ishidate

Hidehiro Kinoshita

Takao Kubo

Mariko Mori

Takashi Murakami

Rika Takahashi

Satoru Tamura

Kaori Yamamoto

December 2, 2001 to February 3, 2002

Kamloops Art Gallery, Kamloops
British Columbia, Canada

Foreword by   Jann L.M. Bailey
Preface by   Susan Edelstein
Essays by   Kevin Ei-ichi De Forest
              Monika Kin Gagnon
              Professor Yoichi Kimura

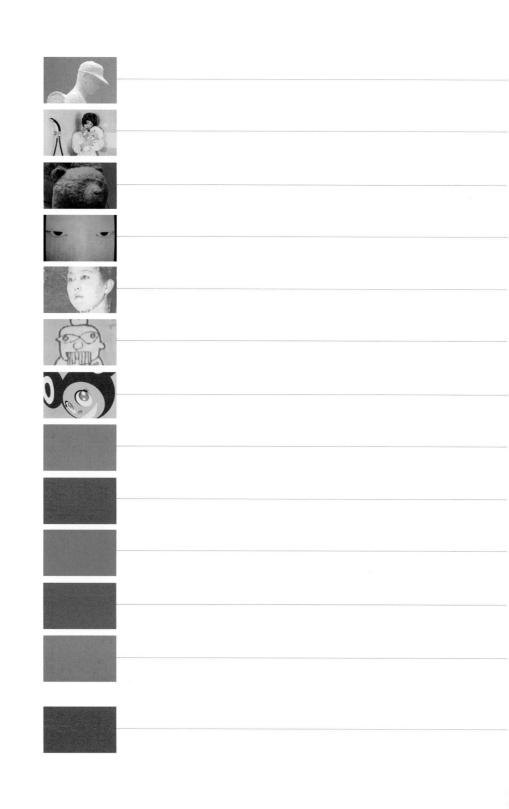

CONTENTS

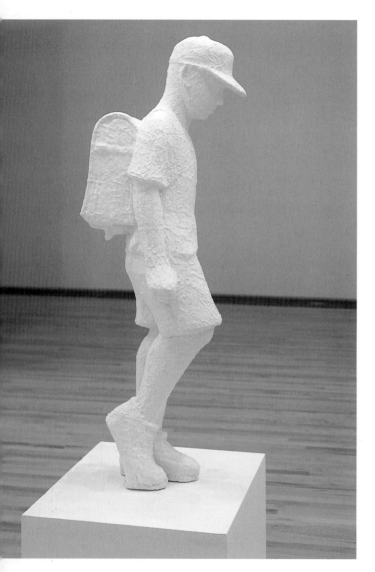

Rika Takahashi
Parallel, 2001

Kaori Yamamoto
Room of Love series, 1997

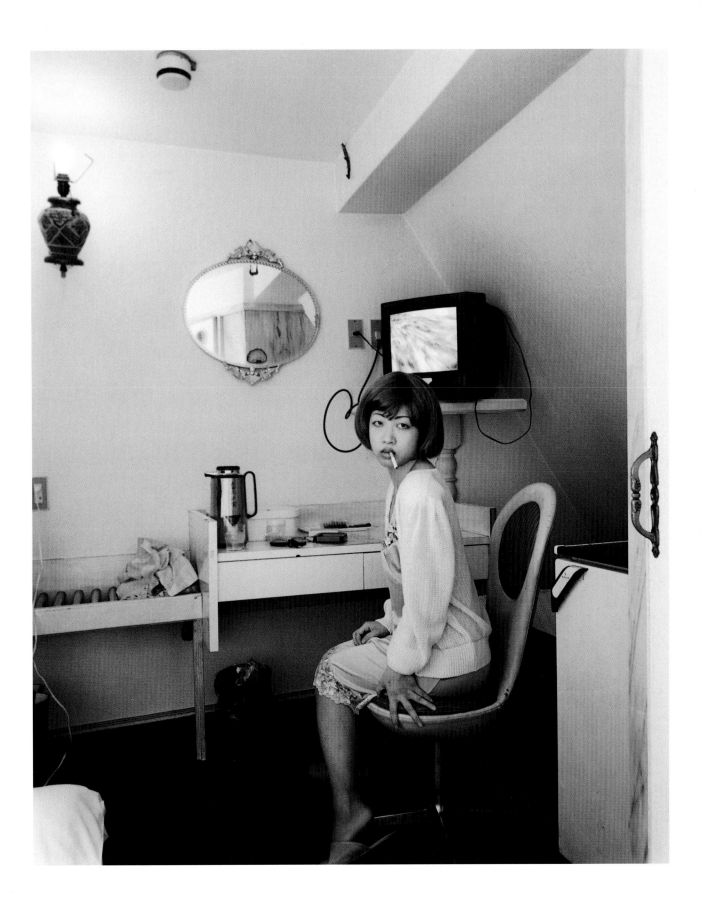

Satoru Tamura
Standing Bears Go Back, 1998

Centre Gallery

Satoru Tamura
The Plastic Models Break Into Pieces, 2000

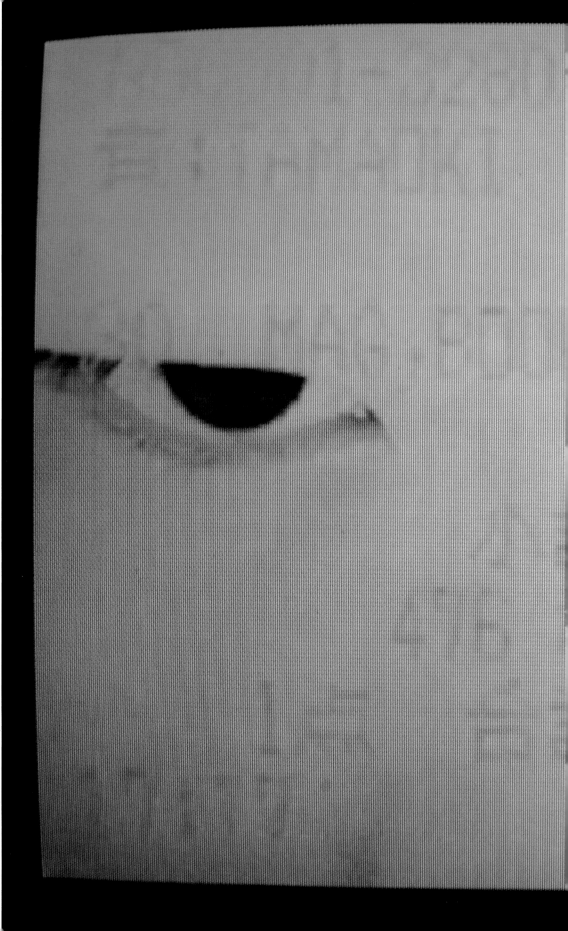

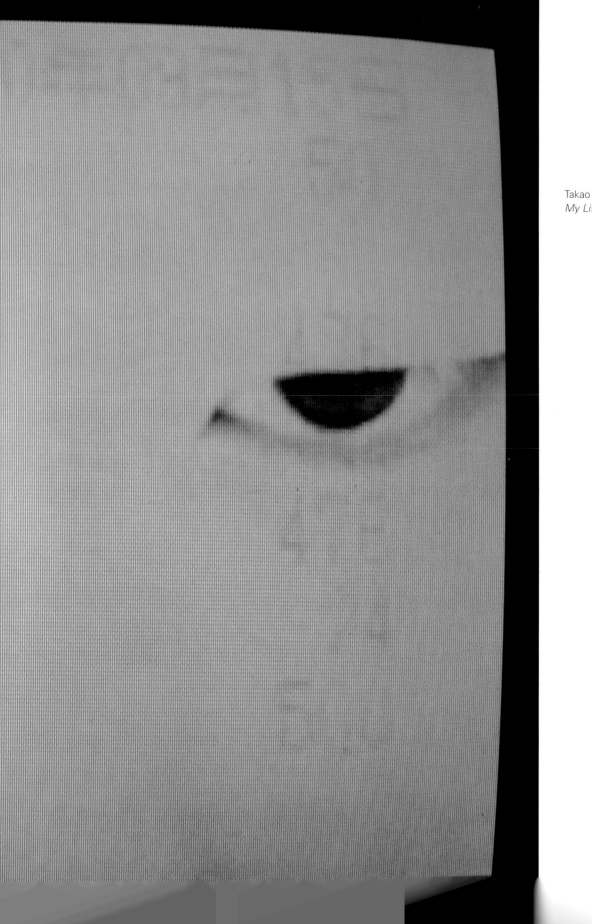

Takao Kubo
My Life, 1999

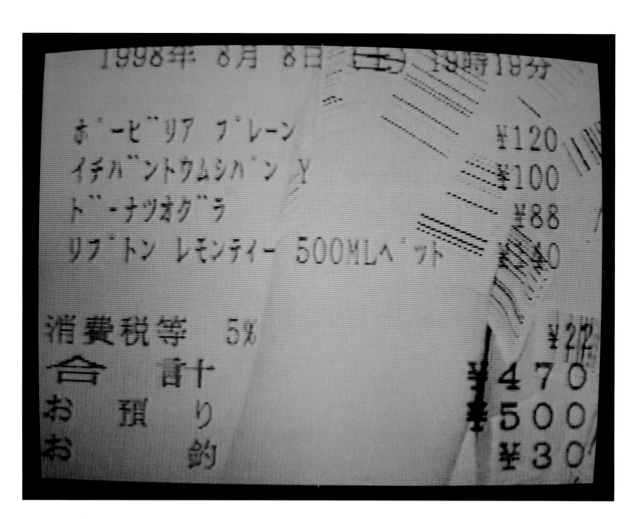

Takao Kubo
My Life, 1999

```
98年 05月 11日      責 382  N/C601
 4564   CD ロック              2,290
 4564   CD ロック D            2,500
 [税対象額                     4,790]
        税 5%                    239
     合 計 2点                5,029
   現  金                     5,050
   釣  銭                       21
17:89                        #0088
```

Mariko Mori
Kumano, 1997-1998

Mariko Mori
Kumano, video still, 1998
Courtesy Deitch Projects, NY
& Gallery Koyanagi, Tokyo

Taichi Ishidate & Hidehiro Kinoshita
Non-interactive: A Meal and I, 2000

Taichi Ishidate & Hidehiro Kinoshita
Non-interactive: A Meal and I, 2000

Takashi Murakami
AND THEN Red, 1999
AND THEN Pink, 1999
AND THEN Yellow, 1999
AND THEN Blue, 1999
AND THEN Light Blue, 1999

Takashi Murakami
Kerotan, 2001 (this page)
DOB Jump, 1999 (opposite)

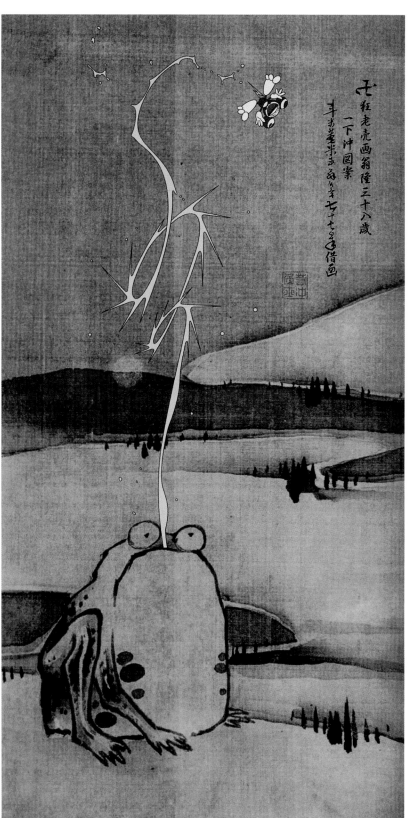

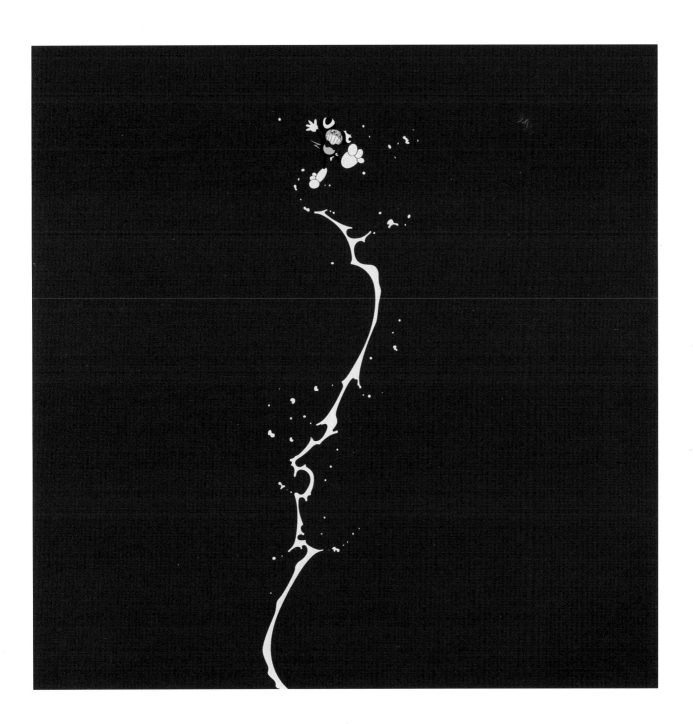

KYOZON

Taichi Ishidate

Hideto Kinoshita

Takashi Kubo

Mari Mori

Takashi Murakami

Rika Takahashi

Satoru Tamura

Organized by Kamloops Art Gallery
December 2 - February 2002
Sponsored in part by British Columbia Lottery Corporation
and Kirin Brewery Company Limited.
Financial assistance received from the Japan-Canada fund, a gift
to The Canada Council for the Arts from the Government of Japan.

Works in the exhibition

Rika Takahashi
Parallel, 2001
glue, paste, pulp from recycled
milk cartons
seven sculptures, each 129 x 40 x 51 cm
Collection of the artist

Kaori Yamamoto
Room of Love series, 1997
18 black and white photographs
nine @ 60.8 x 50.8 cm
one @ 60.8 x 49.5 cm
three @ 45.7 x 55.7 cm
one @ 55.7 x 45.7 cm
one @ 53.5 x 45.2 cm
one @ 54 x 43.5 cm
one @ 49.5 x 43.4 cm
one @ 35 x 45.8 cm
Collection of the artist

Satoru Tamura
Both works collection of the artist

Standing Bears Go Back, 1998
mixed media installation
250 cm x 1800 cm x 150 cm installed

The Plastic Models Break Into Pieces,
2000
video
2 minutes

Takao Kubo
My Life, 1999
video
57 seconds
Collection of the artist

Mariko Mori
Kumano, 1997-1998
video
13 minutes, 27 seconds
Collection of the artist

**Taichi Ishidate &
Hidehiro Kinoshita**
Non-interactive: A Meal and I, 2000
video
7 minutes, 10 seconds
Collection of the artists

Takashi Murakami
All works courtesy of Marianne
Boesky Gallery, New York

DOB Jump, 1999
screenprint, edition 13/50,
40 x 40 cm

PUKAPUKA, 1999
screenprint, edition 25/50,
55.3 x 36.2 cmv

72727, 2001
color laser print, edition 76/105,
41.9 x 29.2 cm

Kerotan, 2001
colour laser print, edition 76/105,
41.9 x 29.2 cm

Manji-fuji, 2001
color laser print, edition 76/105,
29.2 x 41.9 cm

AND THEN Red, 1999
screenprint, edition 49/50,
40 x 40 cm

AND THEN Pink, 1999
screenprint, edition 48/50,
40 x 40 cm

AND THEN Yellow, 1999
screenprint, edition 48/50,
40 x 40 cm

AND THEN Blue, 1999
screenprint, edition 15/50,
40 x 40 cm

AND THEN Light Blue, 1999
screenprint, edition 48/50,
40 x 40 cm

Foreword

Jann LM Bailey
Director
Kamloops Art Gallery

The artists represented in *Kyozon* have explored the enigmatic issues of identity, place, and popular culture with careful consideration of the synthesis of East and West, as well as their own positions within this complex landscape. This exhibition provides a unique perspective on contemporary Japan, a reflection of the issues and ideas which define a specific time and place.

I would like to thank the artists, Taichi Ishidate, Hidehiro Kinoshita, Takao Kubo, Mariko Mori, Takashi Murakami, Rika Takahashi, Satoru Tamura, and Kaori Yamamoto, for their participation in this important exhibition.

I was delighted when Susan Edelstein, Curator of the Kamloops Art Gallery, first broached the subject of organizing an exhibition from Japan as I felt it would resonate throughout our community and generate much discussion. I congratulate her on organizing this important exhibition and thank her for her hard work and thorough search for and selection of the artists.

A partnership was formed with the University College of the Cariboo whereby Japanese exchange student Shima Iuchi participated, as part of a credited university course, in the initial stage of research both in Japan and in Kamloops. I would like to extend our thanks to Iuchi for her dedication, time and hospitality while Edelstein was in Japan.

I would also like to acknowledge Monika Kin Gagnon, Kevin Ei-ichi De Forest, and Professor Yoichi Kimura, who have written texts for the exhibition catalogue. Judith Steedman has designed a handsome publication, and I would like to thank her and also Kim Clarke for his expert photographic work on this project.

We have gained a number of new friends in Japan whose assistance with the logistics surrounding an exhibition of this scope bears recognition. On behalf of the Board of Trustees of the Kamloops Art Gallery, I would like to extend sincere thanks to them, especially Makiko Hara and Hideko Iuchi, for their gracious assistance with this project.

Several staff members of the Kamloops Art Gallery have been directly involved in the organization of the exhibition. I would like to acknowledge the work of Trish Keegan, Beverley Clayton and Erin Moen.

British Columbia Lottery Corporation and Kirin Brewery Company have kindly sponsored this exhibition, supporting both the organization of the exhibition and individual artists. BCLC's generous contributions have enabled us to present workshops facilitated by members of the Kamloops Japanese Canadian Association in Kamloops and to include entertainment by the Uzume Taiko Drummers of Vancouver at the opening reception.

The Kamloops Art Gallery is generously supported by The Canada Council for the Arts, with an additional Japan-Canada Fund grant for this exhibition, the Museums Assistance Program of the Department of Canadian Heritage, the British Columbia Arts Council, the City of Kamloops, and the Gallery sponsors, donors and members. Our sincere and continued appreciation is extended for this financial assistance.

Preface: Rigid Borders, Porous Boundaries

Curator
Kamloops Art Gallery

In the tradition of *Kabuki*, Japanese theatre characterized by elaborate costumes and male actors in all the roles, there is a brilliant process of transformation that occurs while the play is in progress. The process is called *Hikinuki*, which means "pulling out the threads." This flawless transformation occurs when a stagehand, known as a *Koken*, facilitates a costume change before a live audience. The Koken traditionally carries on and removes all stage properties and scenery during the course of the performance. Dressed in black, the *Koken* strategically blends into the darkness of the set where he works at pulling out the eight threads that hold the actor's outer garment together. Once all the threads are out, the *Koken* pulls off the actor's kimono to reveal a new costume, and the transformation is complete. All of this is done while the actor is dancing.

Kyozon is my curatorial *Hikinuki*: an exhibition in which I have attempted to gently tease apart and pull out the surface threads in order to gain a deeper understanding of contemporary culture in Japan. Working with the eight artists, whose careers fall into categories of either emerging or established, I gradually discovered overlapping concerns in their work. None of this would have been possible without the keen interest and generosity of the artists, Taichi Ishidate, Hidehiro Kinoshita, Takao Kubo, Mariko Mori, Takashi Murakami, Rika Takahashi, Satoru Tamura, and Kaori Yamamoto, who allowed me to carefully pull at the threads of their culture, one by one.

The importing and exporting of cultures and value systems has become a dominant discourse in both academic and vernacular circles, and it strikes me that this exchange occurs on a number of levels and to different ends. As simple as importing culture over the Internet or as complex as political conflict on a global scale, the homogenization of cultures has become a ripe area for exploration. At what point does the exchange become an imposition of one culture at the expense of another?

Eating sushi in a restaurant in Kamloops, British Columbia, seems perfectly natural to me, but drinking an americano at Starbucks in Tokyo felt strangely (un)comfortable. This type of cross-cultural exchange became the impetus for researching the works for the exhibition. Along with the residual effects of popular culture, I questioned more than gender and race, examining instead the limits of authenticity and ownership. This conflation of culture, both within Japan and beyond its borders to the West, seemed to exist almost as seamlessly as the availability of a Starbucks coffee. It was the blend of traditional Japanese culture, contemporary Japanese culture, and contemporary Western culture that became the focus of the exhibition. This was the basis for the development of what would become *Kyozon*, which means "merging or bringing together of opposite things."

In early 2000 I made my first trip to Japan, where I spent much of my time observing my surroundings and attempting to stay within the confines of proper protocol. In the world of academia and contemporary art practice, the critique around globalization and cultural homogenization continues to be debated. Like a voyeur, I started doing studio visits in 2000, hoping to formulate my own conclusions on the globalization phenomenon.

In the spring of 2001 I completed my second excursion to Japan, this time feeling far more at ease and able to concentrate on the art works rather than my being in Japan. As a foreign guest I was treated with extreme regard. Many people went out of their way to accommodate me. Despite all of this generosity it quickly became apparent to me that as a woman, especially as a foreign woman, my experiences and access to various worlds within Japan would be limited. Any time one travels, awkward or difficult situations can arise, especially when a different language is part of the equation. However, language was not my only barrier. I had become, if only for a brief moment in the span of my privileged life, the "other." My "otherness" prevented me from penetrating spaces, such as the Gion, the area that houses the compounds in which Geisha and *Maiko* (a young woman training to become a Geisha) study and live. This excluded position was new to me, and my florid complexion and red hair became an inescapable veneer. My North American-size physique made me easily recognizable, even in a dense crowd. Lumbering through Tokyo, I began to feel exotically (in)visible, conscious that in comparison to a Japanese woman, I was as delicate as a Sumo wrestler. I began to understand that emulating the *Koken* could take years of practice, and pulling out the eight threads would not be an easy task.

While Japan is known as a land of contrasts, old versus new, tranquility versus frenetic activity, there seems to be a magical kind of melding that goes on, blending the hectic pace of its large cities with the meditative serenity of its temples and gardens. In retrospect, one of the most memorable contrasts I observed was of a *Maiko* dressed in full regalia, having a discussion on a cell phone. While I was in Japan this didn't really seem to be out of the ordinary, but in hindsight, this type of encounter was just one more of the dichotomies I experienced.

Japan comes alive at night, but only if you know where to look. Behind the safety of closed doors one can commonly see the regimented businessman of the day shed his corporate persona as he partakes in the evening ritual of karaoke. Becoming a temporary pop-star at the local bar is a routine way to relax.

Contemporary culture co-exists with the strict protocol of traditional culture, and within this co-existence the sex-trade is discreetly acknowledged as a way to satisfy a "natural urge" and is openly advertised and available to businessmen in the privacy of "Love Hotels." These castle-like structures are easily recognized in the urban landscape and represent a refuge from the stress of daily life. The rooms of these hotels offer fantasy décor. A man can rent a room by the hour or for a whole night. Payment is requested in advance and the transaction is administered in the most unobtrusive manner possible. After a room is selected, payment is facilitated through an automated system. Interacting with the cool metal lips of a vending machine, the client is rewarded with a room key. All of this is done without the client ever being confronted by another human being.

At the close of the Japanese business day, well-groomed men in suits, accompanied by sexy young women, "work" the busier train stations. The women, whispering "sexy, sexy," openly solicit clients from travelling groups of inebriated businessmen, while their male counterparts recruit other young women to work in the hotels. Although the cultural phenomenon of the Love Hotel is never openly discussed, everyone in Japan knows it exists.

Japan is densely populated and suffers from an extreme land shortage. This lack of physical space tends to make everything in Japan feel that much more intimate. Japan is about the same size as the state of California. Eighty percent of the country is mountainous and therefore uninhabitable. Recent statistics show Japan's population to be approximately 126 million, all living within an area of 377,835 square kilometers. Canada, in comparison, has a small population of 30.6 million contained within an area of 9,970,610 square kilometers. Estimates show that by 2025 Japan will have roughly one elderly person for every two persons of working age, which will give it a higher old-age dependency ratio than any other major industrial country in the world.

By pulling at the threads of culture, I was able to explore some of the concerns and ideas of a younger generation of artists. While there is no doubt that an East/West exchange exists, a certain amount of transformation occurs in transit. While globalization may be making Western and Eastern audiences familiar with each other's culture, a great deal is altered in the transfer between cultures, contrary to the idea of homogenization and global compression.

From a Japanese perspective the works in *Kyozon* may not seem highly political, especially, as Professor Yoichi Kimura points out, in comparison to earlier contemporary movements that occurred in Japan during the 1960s and '70s. However, to an outsider like me, these works are highly charged with political significance, revealing a social structure and day-to-day reality quite different from those of most North American artists. Strategizing to cope with problems of physical space, lack of financial support, and the regimented nature of corporatisation and cultural protocol has forced artists in Japan to work in very different ways. So, while Sumo wrestling, karaoke and Japanese comic-inspired superheroes are part of Western popular culture, they are still very much the authentic creation of Japan.

This catalogue is the result of the work of many talented individuals to whom I would like to express my gratitude. A very special thanks to Jann L.M. Bailey, Director of the Kamloops Art Gallery, for her ongoing enthusiasm and support of this project. Trish Keegan, Registrar, Erin Moen, Curatorial Administrative Assistant, and Beverley Clayton, Administrative Assistant, all helped in numerous ways to make this project a success, especially in compiling this publication. I thank Kim Clarke for capturing the essence of this exhibition photographically and Judith Steedman of Steedman Design for her sensitive and meticulous work on this publication.

I am indebted to the three writers who embraced this project: long-time associate Monika Kin Gagnon, Kevin Ei-ichi De Forest, and Professor Yoichi Kimura contributed informed, provocative texts. A literal translation of Yoichi Kimura's text from Japanese into English was provided by Yoshie Ozawa, and editing of the translation was provided by Erin Moen and Trish Keegan.

Many people beyond the Kamloops Art Gallery have been closely associated with the realization of the exhibition: Shima Iuchi, who initially invited me to Japan, worked as my research assistant, translator and tour guide during my first trip to Japan; Makiko Hara worked as my assistant and translator during my second trip in 2001; free-lance curator Musashi Ogura was very generous during my stay; Jeffrey Deitch and the staff of Deitch Projects, New York; Jay Sanders and the staff of Marianne Boesky Gallery, New York; Hideko Iuchi, Hitoshi and Hitomi Iuchi, Chizu Motooka, Taito Motooka, Yuriko Hayashi, Nagako Hayashi, Akira and Eiko Hibino and the rest of the Hibino family; Hideki Sekine, Professor of Fine Art, Wakoh University; Akira Shintani and Kenichi Horii, Uji City Hall; Tohru Tanabe, President of Seian University; Donald Lawrence, Associate Professor of Fine Arts, University College of the Cariboo; Lois Rugg, Production Technician, Media Services, UCC; Bryan Best, Lee Kenney, and Grant Thurgood; Gary McCall, Kamloops Fire Department; Betty Inouye, Roy Inouye, Sally Arai and the volunteers of the Kamloops Japanese Canadian Association; Brian Mullvihill, a.k.a. Trolley Bus; the members of the Vancouver Urasenke School of the Japanese Tea Ceremony; Grace Thompson, Director of Japanese Canadian National Museum, Burnaby, B.C.; Patrik Andersson for his contributions to the panel discussion; and Trevor Eglington.

Financial assistance from the Japan-Canada Fund, a gift to the Canada Council for the Arts from the Government of Japan, British Columbia Lottery Corporation and Kirin Brewery Company Limited is greatly appreciated.

Finally, I would like to thank the eight artists who accepted my invitation to participate in *Kyozon*. It has been both a pleasure and a privilege to work with them and to present their work at the Kamloops Art Gallery.

The artists featured in the exhibition *Kyozon* are the cultural offspring of the eclectic history of the Japanese art world, and their works are best considered with an understanding of the social conditions that informed their development.

In December 1969, I became the editor of the monthly art magazine *Mizue*, published by Bijutsu Shuppansha. My position allowed me access to some of the most influential people and events in the arts, and through them I was able to contextualize and better understand what was happening around me.

As my first assignment at *Mizue*, I spent two weeks in Osaka, covering the "International Symposium of Iron Sculpture," which was held concurrently with the Expo '70 OSAKA. At the symposium, I met for the first time such renowned sculptors as Philip King, Jean Tinguely, George Rickey, and Kenneth Snelson, most of whom were staying in Osaka to work on their exhibits. During the day I interviewed the artists while they worked on their exhibits at rented iron factories, and in the evening we would return to the hotel to debate issues in modern art. Those discussions over dinner and drinks with foreign and Japanese artists were invaluable, giving me insights I could never have learned from books.

They talked about many issues, first as human beings, then as artists. The exciting discussions continued each night, with artists from distant places bringing forth topics of preoccupation in their homelands. The artists from Europe talked about Catholicism and about Socialism in the Soviet Union. The Americans compared European cultures to their own. Those from Japan discussed the conflict and fusion between the traditional Japanese arts and modern art.

Six months later, during the World Expo of 1970, many young artists, most of whom were unknown in Japan, gathered at the Tokyo Municipal Museum of Arts to attend the 10th Tokyo Biennnale. "Between Man and Matter" was organized by art critic Yusuke Nakahara and sponsored by the Mainichi Press.

Among those artists were Daniel Buren, Christo, Barry Flanagan, Jannis Kounellis, Sol Lewitt, Mario Merz, Panamarenko, Klaus Limke, and Richard Serra. At the time, the only names I recognized were Christo and Panamarenko, the latter an experimental Belgian artist just emerging onto the global art scene. This group's approach was to exhibit materials in their original forms, rather than in the traditional method of expressing feeling through art. I remember the jarring effect of seeing their work for the first time. The stark presentation of natural materials, such as rocks, iron and paper, on the museum floor without any refinement or processing was refreshing. In my mind, this heralded a new era in the arts.

About the same time as the 10th Tokyo Biennnale, a group of artists, later referred to as the "School of Physical Matter," was exhibiting at many galleries throughout Tokyo. They rejected the traditional process of expressing the relationships between one's own ideas and the object, but rather allowed the subject matter to stand on its own.

I think this movement had already begun by the time of the 10th Tokyo Biennale. The new group of artists did not organize intentionally, but formed naturally in resistance to the traditional conventions of modern art, such as the wasteful fads being created at the time. I don't believe that these artists had communicated with one another or declared their artistic intentions publicly, but rather met by chance at the Tokyo exhibition.

The "Matter Group" was highly influential in Japan during the 1970s. This influence proved mutually beneficial to the increasingly minimalist modern art movement and the artists themselves. Artists were free to develop their own individual styles. More significant than this individual evolution, however, was the evolution of the arts as a whole. Artists studied the changing art scene and responded. In the late 1970s, an international cluster of young artists produced paintings influenced by neo-expressionism. The strong brushstrokes, jolting colours, and distortion of forms that characterized the style represented a backlash against early 1970s minimalism and conceptual arts, which many found exclusive and difficult to understand. Because of this difficulty the art of the early '70s flourished only within the arts community and lacked appeal to the general public.

Elsewhere, German expressionism, prevalent from 1910-1930, persisted, especially in East Germany. This was evident in the exhibition of paintings in the late 1970s until the beginning of the 1980s in East Berlin, the meeting place of East and West Germany. Expressionistic art in Italy sought an escape from the influence of Catholicism and instead reminisced about the spirit of the Roman Empire. In America, many young, newly discovered European artists arrived in New York and were influenced by the heightened attention to ethnic considerations. This energy added momentum to the new expressionism.

Tadanori Yokoo, an outstanding Japanese graphic designer, entered the art scene at the beginning of the 1980s. Yokoo was unsatisfied with the uninspiring paintings he saw in Tokyo. For him, they mimicked the mainstream trend of minimalism. He responded by creating huge, powerful paintings with an unorthodox blend of colours and objects, drawing on his experience as a graphic designer. His awareness of the spread of the new expressionism in Germany, Italy and New York was evident in his early work. His work, however, was not accepted by the Japanese art world. It was only due to a strong following among young Japanese that his work was welcomed by the fashion and music industries. Yokoo's crossover from the world of graphic design into fine art forced those insulated within the art world to open their eyes to the larger, outside world.

Shinro Otake reached significant status in Japan during the same period as Yokoo. After giving up his pursuit of an art degree, he went to England and befriended David Hockney, the renowned British painter, draftsman, and printmaker. On his return to Japan in the 1980s, he created works based on his interpretation of expressionism. During his time in London he became interested in the punk rock subculture. Young punk rock musicians and those in the fashion industry recognized this influence in his work and became interested in his art and his lifestyle.

Yokoo and Otake were two artists who expanded the boundaries of the Japanese art world, a world previously restricted by conventional intelligence and reason. Innovators such as Yokoo and Otake created an atmosphere in which 'outsiders' were empowered to enjoy the arts, marking a significant change to the former exclusivity of fine art in Japan.

At the beginning of the 1990s, the Japanese art scene experienced major changes. Modern art seemed to focus on young people up to the mid-20s age group, as artistic production was based largely on daily events and environments experienced by the younger generation. This may be attributed to the void that Yokoo and Otake left in the arts when they violated the strict conventions that had guided Japanese artists before them. The changing priorities of artists demonstrated a fundamental shift in attitude: anyone was free to enjoy art, whether for the social and political message it conveyed or simply for its visual appeal.

This shift in attitude meant that ordinary events were now also meaningful to artists, not just to 'ordinary' people. The young artists participating in *Kyozon* developed their skills working in this environment.

The theme of daily life runs throughout Takao Kubo's work. The young, emerging artist sees mundane events, such as going to the convenience store or fast food restaurant near his apartment, as areas worthy of artistic exploration. He shops, eats modestly, and pays his bills, saving the receipts of these transactions as a kind of record of his daily life. His situation is not unique: most young people of his generation live more or less the same way. His work is not angry, but rather accepting of the reality of consumer existence, and it encourages us to look closely at our own uneventful daily lives.

The work done by Taichi Ishidate and Hidehiro Kinoshita, two artists who began working together at the Seian University of Art and Design, is composed of video images and animation. In contrast to the work of Takao Kubo, Ishidate and Kinoshita manipulate reality, using animated images to symbolize daily life. Their video culminates with a boy watching images of murder and war unfolding outside a surrealistic window. These events are happening elsewhere in the world but appear to be taking place just outside the boy's home. "Real" television images inserted throughout the video show politicians and intellectuals delivering comments as unrealistic as the animated images. But the violent events in the video are viewed from the safe cocoon of a living room, sparing the viewer from direct involvement. The use of animation gives the artists an effective tool for emphasizing the manipulative capabilities of global communication. Through the work of Ishidate and Kinoshita, our thoughtless acceptance of what we see on television is called into question.

Parallel, by Rika Takahashi, brings to mind the work of American sculptor George Segal, whose life-size plaster casts of human figures are aesthetically similar to those of Takahashi.

Also similar to Segal, Takahashi focuses on daily life, but she emphasizes the negative aspects of her elementary school experience. The children in her installation, as in Japanese society generally, are herded into schools to walk aimlessly, heads down, into the endless competition that is life. They are driven by the myth that higher education automatically means a higher standard of living. But the benefits of an ivy league education and employment by a large company can be overturned by a severe economic recession, destroying one's life. Rika Takahashi's work questions the ideals that Japanese society holds dear, weighing the costs of intensely competitive education against the benefits.

Kaori Yamamoto's *Room of Love* series brings to mind the works of famed American photographer Cindy Sherman. Both appear as models in their own photographs, but they differ in that Sherman looks outward to provoke the viewer while Yamamoto's work is introspective. In training her lens on herself Yamamoto proposes self-revelation, but never truly reveals herself. She speaks to the desires of women of her generation and the measures to which they will resort to attain them. Her photographs, like Vermeer's "room" paintings, are not meant to freeze a moving object in a moment in time. They are intended to capture the transformation of the ordinary woman into a special one, with the artist herself acting as the subject of change.

Satoru Tamura's work is unquestionably enjoyable; almost everyone who sees his work smiles. I do not know the artist's intention for this work of three standing bears going forward and backward powered by propellers embedded in their bellies. His work does not, at first, seem to be serious, but the more one sees of it, the more one starts wondering about its possibilities. Tamura's work may indicate a new direction in sculpture, a direction that requires the viewer to both pose questions and formulate answers.

Compared to the other artists whose work is included in *Kyozon*, Mariko Mori is more well-established. She was born in 1967 in Tokyo and, after modeling in her teens, she studied fashion in Tokyo before moving to London in 1988 to attend Chelsey Art School. She then undertook the Independent Study Program at the Whitney Museum of American Arts before creating her own work. She was never involved in Tokyo's art community. After having spent so much of her early life in London and America, it was natural for her to question the meaning of being Japanese. Mori likely faced the dilemma of either following her own desires or acknowledging the co-existence in Japan of traditional Japanese culture with European culture, which was forced by the events of World War II.

Mariko Mori, now one of Japan's most prominent young artists, overcame the negativity of having become established in the absence of Japanese art society and amid the complexities of a hybrid culture. Her work, combining purity and defenselessness, is invaluable to Japanese society for its innocence and timeliness.

Takashi Murakami, the best-known Japanese artist featured in *Kyozon*, has been referred to as the Pop Samurai. The prolific sculptor and painter lives and works part time in New York, allowing him physical distance from the society he critiques. He describes his signature cartoon figure, DOB, as a representation of the negative aspects of Japanese society. DOB is outwardly appealing, but lacks meaning and understanding of life's greater issues. Murakami both critiques and exploits the Japanese obsession with *anime* (animation) and *manga* (cartoons), capitalizing on the popularity of DOB by taking him into the realm of high art and simultaneously immortalizing him in the form of plush dolls, mouse pads, and T-shirts. Three of Murakami's new works, exhibited for the first time in *Kyozon*, feature DOB incorporated into traditional Japanese surroundings, which encapsulates the conflict at the thematic centre of the exhibition.

Kyozon is an exhibition of works by young Japanese artists, some still engaged in the formal study of art and others well into successful careers, commenting on their shared reality. For those on the outside of Japanese society peering in, *Kyozon* provides rare insights into the tensions of a society being tugged in different directions. It represents the concerns of both internationally acclaimed young artists and those just beginning their commentaries on Japanese society, permitting a glimpse into the future of Japanese contemporary art.

Kyozon Video: Consumer Ennui, the Lure of Divinity and the 'Spiritual Marketplace'

Monika Kin Gagnon

1 Masashi Ogura, "Une histoire de l'art contemporain au Japon," *Parachute* 88 (oct/nov/déc 1997): 28. The translation from French is mine; the French reads: "Aux yeux des Occidentaux, le Japon constituait une culture tout à fait différente, avec un double visage : d'un côté, la part irrationelle, primitive et animistique, avec son Zen et son kamikaze; de l'autre, la part modernisée avec ses industries et ses nouvelles technologies."

2 Alexandra Munroe, "Scream Against the Sky," in *Japanese Art After 1945: Scream Against the Sky*, ed. Alexandra Munroe (New York: Abrams, 1994), 20.

3 Makiko Hara, "Contemporary Japanese Art: Young Artists, Consumer Culture and Internationalization," *Parachute* 88 (oct/nov/déc 1997): 36.

Japan's characterization as a technological giant is often placed in stark contrast to its profound depth of tradition and mythology. Witness the cover of *National Geographic*'s coffee table-destined *Then and Now*, in which a traditionally adorned Kyoto geisha conducts a cell phone call in the back seat of a vehicle. As Japanese curator Masashi Ogura described in his brief 1997 essay, "Une histoire de l'art contemporain au Japon": "Through Occidental eyes, Japan constitutes a completely different culture with a dual face: on one side, is the irrational, primitive and animistic part, with its Zen and kamikaze; on the other, its modernized persona, with its industries and new technologies."[1] This tensile paradox of cutting-edge new technologies associated with Western industrialization, and the weight of deep, ancient tradition also finds itself in recent political histories of Japan. The Meiji Restoration of 1868 is often seen as a key turning point in the modernization of Japan, as is the post-1945 American military occupation of Japan that imposed a Western-style democracy. Curator Alexandra Munroe remarks: "The notion that Japanese history is divided at Meiji is most definitive in the field of art history. For the most part, Japanese specialists abroad have neglected late-nineteenth- and twentieth-century art, as if modern Japan, corrupted by Westernization and industrialization, were incapable of creating a significant culture of visual arts that could equal the achievements of the classical past."[2] Montréal-based Japanese curator Makiko Hara further remarks on the effect of these dualities manifesting in curatorial practices and exhibitions as increasing numbers of Japanese artists began appearing on the international scene in the late 1980s. In her essay, "Contemporary Japanese Art: Young Artists, Consumer Culture and Internationalization," Hara paraphrases Japanese photographer Hiroshi Sugimoto, who argues that this "schism" operates "as the difference between the mythic discourse affirming the role of Japanese religions and traditional relations embodied in the former, and a more evidently postmodern discourse, one defined by the tendency toward rapid technological development in later-capitalism, in the latter."[3]

The last decade of artistic production by an emerging generation of artists in Japan, according to Hara, may not be easy to define as distinctively Japanese, given a global art world now characterized less by nationally-bound traditions than by a more multivalent exposure to artists, art educations and exhibitions on an international circuit. Hara's problematizing of the Japanese artist's essential characteristics in the 1980s hints at the implications of a post-national art world, where the organizing principles of nationhood have become increasingly vexed. Interestingly, this poses challenges about how to engage the four video-based works in the exhibition *Kyozon*, curated by Susan Edelstein for the Kamloops Art Gallery, which offers samplings from contemporary Japanese video. Should they be faithfully situated within their immediate cultures of production? Or viewed as videotexts detached from the specificity of their cultural emergence? Further, does one read this exhibition as an instance of *inter*-cultural exchange between Japan and Canada that respects a cultural difference based on these

4 Quoted in Carol S. Eliel, "Interpreting Tradition: Mariko Mori's *Nirvana*" in *Mariko Mori* (Chicago and London: the Museum of Contemporary Art and the Serpentine Gallery, 1998), 28.

5 See, for instance, Martha Rosler's spirited account, "Video: Shedding the Utopian Moment," in *Illuminating Video*, eds. Doug Hall and Sally Jo Fifer (New York: Aperture and Bay Area Video Coalition, 1990), 45.

6 Barbara J. London, ed., *Video from Tokyo to Fukui and Kyoto* (New York: Museum of Modern Art, 1979), Barbara London, *New Video: Japan* (New York: The American Federation of the Arts, 1985), and Barbara London, "X: Experimental Film and Video," in *Japanese Art After 1945: Scream Against the Sky*, ed. Alexandra Munroe (New York: Abrams, 1994), 284-305.

7 London, "X," 291.

boundaries of nation? Or is it *trans*cultural, denoting an erosion of national boundaries in global culture, and therefore simply read 'from here'?

These videoworks encompass three emerging artists exhibiting outside Japan for the first time — Takao Kubo, Taichi Ishidate and Hidehiro Kinoshita — as well as Satoru Tamura, and New York-based Mariko Mori, who has participated in numerous major international exhibitions. The three video shorts may be loosely seen as engaging the contemporary intersection of consumption and everyday life. Takao Kubo's *My Life* (1999) invites us to consider, "How much is my life?" in his two-minute short reflecting on consumer culture. Taichi Ishidate and Hidehiro Kinoshita's *Non-Interactive: A Meal and I* (2000) cleverly juxtaposes a youthful male wandering within urban and domestic scenes that have been line-drawn and animated. Satoru Tamura has contributed *The Plastic Models Break into Pieces* (2000), a two-minute short depicting the demolition of several small plastic models. Mariko Mori's *Kumano* most explicitly plays with the tensions of tradition and modernity in Japan as embedded in a specific historical Buddhist site and her conjuring of three deities within it. Of this tension, Mori has commented: "My interest is not just looking back to traditional ideas or culture. I try to take in not only the present…I try to develop my own future vision and utopian ideas—my own interpretations of tradition."[4]

A consideration in discussing these videos is to briefly engage the historical context of Japanese video art production. Japan's unique contribution to a 40-year international history of video art is the legacy of electronics giant Sony, and its production of the now infamous Portapak in the mid-1960s, the first portable video camera and recording equipment, that quickly captured artists' imaginations. The introduction of the first Portapak to the U.S. in 1965 by Tokyo-based, Korean-born artist and musician Nam June Paik is now deeply mythologized in American video history.[5] On numerous occasions, Museum of Modern Art video curator Barbara London has written in English on the history of Japanese video for different programming events in the U.S. In both 1979 and 1985, London programmed Japanese video artists in New York, and in 1994, she contributed an essay to the accompanying book of the large inter-disciplinary touring exhibition *Japanese Art After 1945: Scream Against the Sky*.[6] In this most recent and extensive essay on electronic arts, London narrates a descriptive chronological history, replete with various artists, events, and general tendencies in video production, including the formation of collectives (Video Hiroba, Video Earth, the Video Information Center, and Image Forum), early experiments with multiple monitors, and film and video projections on *washi*, or Japanese paper. Her starting point is a 1968 event entitled "Say Something Now, I'm Looking for Something to Say," which was organized by critic Tono Yoshiaki and artist Yamaguchi Katsuhiro.[7] She also describes how Canadian video artist Michael Goldberg of the Vancouver video centre, Video Inn, visited Tokyo in 1972 and was surprised with how "little organization" there was in the video scene. Goldberg and video artists

Fujiko Nakaya and Yamaguchi Katsuhiro organized workshops and an exhibition, "Video Communications: Do-It-Yourself Kit," out of which grew a thirteen-member collective, Video Hiroba. Numerous video genres can be seen emerging across Japan in video's early phases: Nakaya's social activist video *Friends of Minamata Victims* (1972), Fukui-based Yamamoto Keigo's video formalism, Idemitsu Mako's distinctive documentary-influenced recordings of domestic life, such as *Another Day in the Life of a Housewife* (1978), and the literary video genre of the "most lauded Japanese videotape," *Video Letter* (1982) by well-known poets Tanikawa Shuntaro and Terayama Shuji. London suggests that by the mid-1980s, interdisciplinary approaches, including the use of video and other electronic media in conjunction with other artistic forms, such as dance and theatre, are best exemplified by the Kyoto arts collective, Dumb Type, formed in 1984, with performance/installations engaging popular culture, such as *Pleasure Life* (1987-88), *pH* (1990-91) and *S/N* (1993-94).

It is within this broad sense of Japan's video art production that we might begin to view the three single-channel works produced by Japanese-born and Japan-based artists. In Kubo's *My Life*, a body is stripped bare and covered in *butoh*-like white makeup, creating a skin surface as screen for the projection of sales receipts and other commodities suggested by bar code symbols. In attributing a quantifiable price to his lifetime consumption, Kubo's fast-paced video short also sets into play the question of how a life's value is measured within consumer cultures where material possessions are viewed as evidence of achievement. Kubo's bleached-out images, fast cutting, and pixilated visual effects differ from the home-video feel of Tamura's *The Plastic Models Break into Pieces*, which documents the destruction of several model kit toys. A static camera set on a platform captures a golf club swinging into frame and demolishing six constructed plastic models, one after the other: "transformer"-like creatures, military tanks, a motorcycle and hi-tech plane, are all smashed into pieces against a facing wall, evoking the temporariness and disposability of material commodities in popular culture.

Ishidate and Kinoshita's *Non-Interactive* creates a more sustained reflection on the state of the world and an individual's daily movements and activities within it. Formally, there is a contrast between the simple, line-drawn animation that composes the video's background environments and the live platinum-blonde Japanese male youth that wanders through this animated landscape. These different registers of representation—animation and live-action—underline a sense of discord between corporeal pleasures (the comfort of eating a bowl of noodles, for instance, or the relief of urinating, which immediately garners a coloured rainbow), and the alienation from reality brought on by contemporary life and, more particularly, by television. The voiceover narrates a day in this youth's life as he rises and wonders "What am I going to do today?" Moving through a field of television sets, he comments on the distortion of the TV subjects' heads, which seem "too big," and more quizzically wonders if these are, indeed, really people? Set in contemporary environments, these three videos all engage with

8 Ibid., 296.

9 William Gibson, "My Own Private Tokyo," in *Wired* (September 2001): 119.

10 London. , "X," 296.

modern cultures of consumption in Japan, in different ways evoking a sense of alienation, anxiety and *ennui*.

Barbara London concludes her essay on Japanese video with two interesting observations regarding the specificity of video production in Japan, which are worth returning to here. The first pertains to the permeation of video technologies into everyday Japanese life, which echoes what *Non-Interactive* seems preoccupied by:

> Not only are taxis, trains, elevators, and doctor's waiting rooms equipped with flat-screen televisions showing the news and visual Muzak, but billboard-size video projections of soft drink and fashion commercials that seductively sell a 'life-style' light up thoroughfares in major urban shipping and nightlife districts. Video has become as common and disposable as wooden chopsticks.[8]

London, like Ishidate and Kinoshita's video, alludes to everpresent television and new electronic technologies in public space. This distinctively Japanese characteristic has captured the Western imaginations of filmmakers such as Ridley Scott in the apocalyptic urban landscapes of *Bladerunner*, or more recently, the Wachowski brothers' sci-fi *The Matrix* with its hybrid cultures that have Asian martial arts and philosophies at their core. William Gibson's novel *Neuromancer* was largely staged in a futuristic Japan, and on his recent return visit to Japan, framed by the question, "Is Japan still the future?" Gibson commented that, indeed, Japan was "Home at last, in the 21st century."[9]

London's second concluding remark concerns the specific conditions of production and dissemination of video art in Japan, which she suggests do not differ markedly from other industrialized countries, despite these visually saturated public spaces. If anything, both government and corporate support of new technology-based, electronic arts culture has been conservative, focusing instead on "'national living treasures' who practice traditional crafts or established forms of theater."[10] However, despite major electronics corporations such as Sony, Matsushita, and Sharp, which are constantly developing the most recent in video and electronic technologies, video artists have not necessarily found easier or cheaper access to video equipment and post-production facilities.

Mariko Mori's *Kumano* (1997-98) presents a video installation by an artist engaging with photography and video for almost a decade, but in her case, as part of a larger multi-disciplinary *oeuvre* that has come to also encompass performance, hi-tech sculptural elements, as well as video in multi-channel installations, projections and recently, 3-D formats. Mori's practice is, in fact, deeply implicated in employing new technologies of various kinds, many of which are developed in relation with various electronics companies:

> In Tokyo, Mori's 'studio' is a euphemism for digital editing suites, laboratories,

11 Lisa Corrin, "Mariko Mori's Quantum *Nirvana*," in *Mariko Mori* (Chicago and London: the Museum of Contemporary Art and the Serpentine Gallery, 1998), 21.

12 Dominic Molon, "Countdown to Ecstasy," in *Mariko Mori* (Chicago and London: the Museum of Contemporary Art and the Serpentine Gallery, 1998), 5.

13 The various photographs being discussed here are reproduced in various publications, including: *Parkett* 54 (1998), *Mariko Mori* (Chicago and London: the Museum of Contemporary Art and the Serpentine Gallery, 1998), and *Japanese Photography: Desire and Void*, eds. Peter Weiermair and Lucas Gehrmann, trans. John S. Southard (Zurich: Edition Stemmle, 1997), 83–87.

and corporate boardrooms where she goes to describe her ideas to inventors who then deploy, accommodate, or create technologies to realize them. The 3-D video system, for example, was specially created by the GIT Corporation to synchronize sound and images in *Nirvana. Dream Temple* will be produced with the aid of Sony....[11]

Mori's formation as an artist includes Bunka Fashion College in Tokyo in the late '80s, art schools in London and New York, punctuated by stints as a fashion model, before she began exhibiting her art works in the early '90s. Her early photography demonstrates the influences of these combined formations, as she models in various futuristic and mythic costumed persona amid urban backdrops that become dramatically transformed by her presence. Her appearance within her own photographs and her playfulness with visual codes of femininity have provoked comparisons to American artist Cindy Sherman, as well as photographer Yasumasa Morimura, who inserts himself into famous reconstructed scenes of spectacular femininity from art history to pop culture. Kaori Yamamoto's self-portraits in *Kyozon* are also an additional point of intersection. In *Subway* (1994), *Tea Ceremony III* (1994), *Play with Me* (1994) and *Last Departure* (1996), Mori is fashioned in her own creations characterized by the futuristic sheen of silver spandex and fiberglass, posed amongst regular bystanders and passers-by in various Tokyo locales, including the subway, and amongst office towers. Curator Dominic Molon effectively describes the idiosyncratic convergences that Mori captures in these early photographs: "Mori's transformation combines such dissonant elements as Japanese tradition, science fiction, and performance art in a singularly spectacular presence."[12] In *Empty Dream* (1995), Mori is costumed as a mermaid lounging on a busy artificial beach, donning a giant tail fin, sparkling sequined bodice and blue ponytail and bangs (the backdrop is, in fact, the world's largest all-weather indoor water park, Ocean Dome, in the Miyazaki prefecture in Japan).[13] The copious detail and sheer grandeur of this latter image (which measures 12 x 24 feet) is suggestive of the narrative potential of these photographic tableaux and their imaginary personae, anticipating the sensational scenarios of the video installations, of which *Kumano* is one.

In the video installations, *Miko no Inori* (1996) (translated as "Shaman-Girl's Prayer") and *Kumano* (1997-98), and the 3-D video installations, *Nirvana* (1996-97) and later, *Dream Temple* (1999), Mori propels her character repertoire from the early cyber-girls and extra-terrestrials into the realm of neo-Buddhist pop spirituality with fantastic goddesses and deities set in stunning landscapes. *Miko no Inori* marks this transition, as a cyber goddess with platinum hair and glowing eyes engages in a ritualistic performance with a translucent crystal globe set within the post-modern architecture of Narita Airport. Art historian Norman Bryson notes a shift from Mori's earlier photographs' "incarnating the social in her own, versatile body," to the mermaid and video deities now exhibiting a "symptomatic personification: Mori conjures up a body and a scenography for that body that are no longer tied (as in her socialist-realist mode)

14 Norman Bryson, "Cute Futures: Mariko Mori's Techno-Enlightenment," in *Parkett* 54 (1998): 77.

15 Bryson, 80.

16 See the Kumano Field Museum website, http://fumi.eco.wakayama-u.ac.jp/KFM/english/ accessed October 31, 2001. All quotations concerning the actual Kumano region are from this website.

17 Margery King, "Mori Pop," in *Mariko Mori* (Chicago and London: the Museum of Contemporary Art and the Serpentine Gallery, 1998), 39.

to any determinate social milieu."[14] While Mori's photographic characters transform the actual settings of contemporary Tokyo, much like Jean-Luc Godard's sci-fi *Alphaville* (1965) made use of Paris' barren outskirts to partially comment on the banality of suburban lifestyles and sociality, the divine personae of Mori's more recent videos now occupy a strangely conflated space simultaneously holding tradition and futuristic utopias at once. Bryson writes of Mori's work composed of bodies both utopic and of the present: "Mori's tantric vision of the body as composed of flaming energies and radiances may correspond to real conditions of the social economy, while at the same time presenting those conditions in a utopian light, as a transfiguration or *Aufhebung* of flesh and blood into subtle lights and energies."[15]

Kumano is named after the remarkable setting within which it is staged, a Buddhist pilgrimage site founded during the Heian period (800 A.D.), known as the 'Land of Rebirth,' where Ippen Shonin would establish the Jishu sect of Buddhism after achieving enlightenment on its grounds. As described by the Kumano Field Museum, which maintains cultural information and access to the site, the pilgrimage route was historically known as the Kumano *Kodo*, or ancient path, which people have traveled for more than a millennium to bathe in the healing atmosphere of the region. This 'place of healing,' wherein one might come particularly to contemplate the meaning of life and death, is also home to Japan's tallest waterfall, Nachi Falls (measuring 133 meters).

> This is Kumano's most sacred waterfall, and the waterfall itself is considered to be a divine entity. From the waterfall the Pacific Ocean can be seen in the distance. In ancient times the land across the sea was thought to be the land of the afterlife. The waterfall, cutting the forest straight down the middle, is an awe-inspiring sight especially when viewed around midnight, at which time it is said that one can see a 'luminescent darkness' hovering above the falls. [16]

It is in *Kumano*'s staging within this "land of mystery where the visible and invisible worlds meet," that Mori's video first accrues its mystical quality. Playing in the actual setting of Kumano and its spiritual accretions, Mori materializes imaginary divinities that register across multiple representational boundaries. Mori has also commented, "I'm interested in crossing over time. We are living in the present, but the past also exists in the present, and the future also exists in the present."[17]

Kumano opens in a misty forest as a handheld camera peruses amongst trees with varying speeds of camera movement (literally like a fast-forward and reverse effect manipulated in editing). The sound of a single xylophone is soon accompanied by Mori's heavenly chanting voice, creating an otherworldly aural ambiance that permeates throughout the video. Three deities, or goddesses, make their appearances in different locales: a luminous mythic woman wears a white fox fur on her back as she gently flees the pursuing camera and runs off into the forest;

Monika Kin Gagnon

18 Eliel, 28. My italics.

19 Jane Mulcock writes: "The notion of a spiritual supermarket does not conjure up the images of sincerity and serious commitment frequently associated with 'authentic' spirituality: rather, it tends to evoke the superficial materialism that comes to mind for many of us when we reflect on the characteristics of the super-market. The phrase itself seems to sing out of contradiction, and oxymoronic union that whispers constantly about the unholy allegiance of spirituality and capitalism." See Mulcock's "Creativity and Politics in the Cultural Supermarket: synthesizing indigenous identities for the r/evolution of spirit," *Continuum: Journal of Media and Cultural Studies*, vol. 15, no. 2 (2001): 170.

Thank you to Jim Drobnick and Kevin Ei-ichi De Forest for providing exhibition cat-alogues and references, to my mother, Michiko Yajima Gagnon, for translations, to Scott Toguri McFarlane for exquisite editing, and to Susan Edelstein for the generous invitation to par-ticipate in the dialogues around this exhibition.

a second ornately head-dressed and exquisitely kimonoed woman performs a slow, ritualistic ceremony of contemplative movements while facing rocky (Nachi?) waterfalls; and a third woman (seemingly housed in a 3-D animated green temple that precedes her appearance), per-forms a traditional Japanese tea ceremony with opaque instruments, kneeling in modern tunic, silver slacks, and silver-blue wig, as small suspended mirrors float and twinkle around her.

Kumano achieves a credible level of ritual spirituality in these three austere episodes mag-nificently theatricalized for the camera. While one is at once convinced of some esoteric grounding of these scenes in Buddhist ceremony, there are other moments when our beliefs seem impetuously challenged. Are the ideographic symbols that flash between the waterfall goddess' gesture really Japanese *hiragana*, or are they an imaginary language invented by Mori? (They are invented.) Is there a meaning evident in the rapid intercutting between the tea divin-ity's face and a salmon-pink rabbit symbol? (Possibly.) But perhaps the most nagging question: Is this feigned spirituality for real? A clue to this may be rendered from Mori's own character-ization of her practice: "I try to develop my own future vision and utopian ideas—*my own inter-pretations of tradition*."[18] For it is in such statements that we glimpse that sense of Mori's play-fulness with signs and symbols, in this case of ritualized spirituality, in which she has particu-larly come to excel. For Mori, playing in the fields of the divine is to set in motion pregnant meanings that, if not themselves spiritual, at least point us toward the profound desire or quest *for* spiritual meaning.

In casting a nod toward traditional Japanese cultures (with the Kumano site, the kimono attire and post-modern tea ceremony), Mori's works entertain a vast, intangible dimension that brings the past and history into play with the optimism of utopia. This dimension sharply con-trasts with the everyday alienation and ennui experienced in present-day consumer cultures, as considered in *Kyozon*'s other videos, *My Life, Non-Interactive* and *Plastic Models*. Yet, when the promise of utopias and the ennui of materiality are brought together, the spiritual realm seems to beckon as an antidote to the vacuousness of consumption. But, is it so easy to escape the cir-cuits of social economies and hollowness of consumer culture? As *My Life, Non-Interactive* and *Plastic Models* present it, the answer is no. Such are the eerie tensions that *Kumano* engages. For any spiritual insincerity would suggest a succumbing to commodification and, therefore, to the ultimately cynical considerations of a spiritual marketplace.[19]

KYOZON—Co-dependence—New Japanese Artists

Kevin Ei-ichi De Forest

The development in the last few years of a global art community has brought to light a diversity of art worlds formerly overlooked by contemporary Western art media. As biennials and dot com galleries around the world proliferate, so does the realization that the criteria once assumed to apply towards contextualizing and evaluating work is not as cut and dried as it may have once appeared to be.

The fascination of the work in *Kyozon* lies in the cultural agency of its artists as they begin to reflect on a Japan of the twenty-first century. Significantly, this work brings into the gallery a transplanted space referring to a Japanese context that has had little exposure in North America.

My own cross-cultural encounter with Japanese art occurred three years ago when I received a Monbusho scholarship to study at Seika University in my mother's hometown of Kyoto. At first I naively imagined my experience there would be a benign self-exploration into some kind of innate *nihonjinroh* (Japaneseness) I possessed. However, upon my arrival I soon realized how un-Japanese I actually was, as so much of that sense of identity appeared bound to the Japanese language, educational system and geography.

What I gained from that eighteen-month stay was an ongoing re-imagining of what a Japanese identity could be and, in turn, my relation to it as both outsider and partial insider. By the end of my stay, my relativist position towards understanding the kind of cultural difference I was experiencing seemed futile. At times I felt extremely marginalized as a foreigner. I became frustrated by the apparent inability of some Japanese to imagine my having a mixed heritage and this confounded my desire to understand this place that somehow had my identity excluded by definition. That attitude, of a mythical Japanese model of nationalistic purity, is now inadequate as it denies recognition of the growing and hybrid diversity of its subjects.

My position might be seen as imposing a Western perspective on a culture that can't be observed or fully understood in terms other than its own. But Japan is no longer an island unto itself, and, if truly capable of adapting its own culture to foreign influence, it must somehow begin a more profound self-critical evaluation of its relation to the "other," whether that be third generation Koreans still fighting to retain their identity, or inter-marrying Westerners and their *hapa* families. The visual arts is a potential site for this kind of reflexive questioning that, for the Japanese, will finally acknowledge their culture as a dynamic entity in a state of flux, capable of giving voice to those who are disempowered.

At Seika University, this kind of invested cultural critique occurred, but usually through prompting from foreign students. A number of Korean and other Asian students rallied together around issues of discrimination, such as the Japanese denial of the abuse of "comfort women," Korean nationals imprisoned as prostitutes at the service of the Japanese army during World War II. Such a controversial issue is ordinarily swept under the rug and ignored within the conventions of the Japanese system. An acknowledgment of Japan's own failure to speak on its faults towards its marginalized populations has been made, and slowly a critical awareness is appearing among its younger generation.

One of the complexities in following Japan's interrelations with other cultures lies in its ability for skillful mimicry that on the surface might give the appearance of a hybrid exchange. But looks can be deceiving. I was at first impressed, for example, at the punk stylings I'd see on the streets of Osaka's Americamura district, but soon realized this was nothing more than high fashion, something which had nothing at all to do with an original do-it-yourself rebellious stance. But, as with many Japanese versions of Western iconography, what bore a visible verisimilitude at first glance was intentionally left there on the surface, a kind of camouflage that belied the workings of an extremely different mindset.

Japanese industry is renowned for what was once considered a liability: its skill in the copying of Western goods. The resemblance between Western and Japanese cultural products, in popular music styles for example, typically remains on the surface of the product, which is of considerable significance in a culture that places high value on presentation. This semblance can be deceptive, however, since it doesn't necessarily follow that the ideologies behind those signs have been considered at all.

A similar sense of mimicry occurred when I viewed artwork. I always tried to premise my experience with a difficult question: What exactly was it, with the limited experience I had here in Japan, that I was seeing? My own confidence in observing work became unsettled as I realized how much of my own expectations and assumptions had lost their Western frame of reference. Certainly there were the familiar elements of gallery-going—the attendants, the white cube, the silent reverence. But when I noticed a resemblance between a Japanese artist's work and a prominent Westerner's, how could I begin to understand the differences around the perception and value of originality?

To observe the structural differences of the art system in Japan, it should be first noted that Japanese contemporary artists lack the luxury of government support that we have in Canada. There is no parallel gallery system, although artist-run spaces are slowly emerging amongst the commercial galleries. Showing work, however, is usually a costly proposition. Spaces are rented only for a week at a time due to their high real estate value, and the artist is often responsible for all exhibiting expenses. Other notable commercial venues include galleries run by department stores, such as Parco in Tokyo, which draw their young shoppers into cutting edge international exhibitions. The flourishing of large-scale and extravagant contemporary museums has diminished since the recent economic downturn, and many of them predictably gravitate towards the safe bet of established blue-chip artists. In direct monetary contrast, there is also a vibrant underground performance community making use of what little space, either public or private, is left available.

It is also worth noting that many Japanese artists receive attention for their work only after

Kevin Ei-ichi De Forest

1 Masashi Ogura, "Une histoire de l'art contemporain au Japan", *Parachute* No. 88, Oct-Dec 1997: 28.

having proven themselves by success abroad. Perhaps this is a case of attempting to measure the worth of modern art on its own Western terms, but as a career-validating factor for many artists in Japan, it suggests a certain local lack of respect or comprehension. Japan's is an island culture that has traditionally been resistant to change, and the adaptation of the Western trope of Modernism in the visual arts has been the subject of significant debate surrounding Japan's coming to terms with a Western influence on its once "pure" or uncolonized state. The late 1960s saw a Japan that was struggling with its identity as a "colonized" subject of the West, coming to terms with necessary Western modernization and industrialization that was at odds with traditional values. Enormous student riots occurred in protest of the American occupation and Japanese military policy. A number of artists of that generation eloquently defined their "Japaneseness" as negotiating the borderline between a more static Japanese tradition and the impending influence of the West.

The strength of this hybrid exploration was the great risk it took in addressing the hypocrisy of the dominant social order. It is important to acknowledge the relatively subtle and discreet strategies involved in critiquing traditional Japanese values from within. To complicate things further, this was achieved by superimposing a Western model of the avant-garde onto a Japanese system.

The sporadic appearance of Japanese group exhibitions in North America in the late 1980s, such as *A Primal Spirit* and *Against Nature*, described two oppositional tendencies in art-making practice, the former a representation of a Japanese "primitivism" that linked tradition to modernist abstraction, the latter a reflection on Japan's exemplifying a post-modern state of hyper-urbanity. These shows provided a relatively less exoticizing image of Japan to the West, one that has been variously stereotyped in the media as esthetically-refined Zen minimalism, or as bubble-era wealthy purveyors of high technology and glamorous consumerism. Japan was also cited as a working example of post-modern dislocation, which incorrectly assumes it had come to terms with its Western modernist condition in the first place.

The passing of Emperor Hirohito in 1989 signified a new break with the past, and the dichotomy between a link to traditional Japanese "spirituality" and Westernized Japanese modernism became a moot point. According to curator Ogura Masashi, post-industrial Japan has finally exhausted its link with traditional culture, and through this present-mindedness a new generation of artists can choose to reflect directly on their contemporary reality, while others symptomatically retreat into a self-absorbed state of escapism.[1]

Probably the most prominent Japanese artist of the moment both in Japan and abroad is Takashi Murakami, who has championed a youth-culture friendly art as a commodity approach derived from *manga* (Japanese comic strip) imagery. *Manga* is uniquely Japanese in form and crosses all age barriers in readership. At his Hiropon (heroin) Factory complex on the outskirts of Tokyo, Murakami manages his team of comic book artists and craftspeople in the production of paintings, prints and sculptures (as well as more evidently consumable items like key fobs, T-shirts and mouse pads).

He has become somewhat of a celebrity, appearing on a popular television game show, hosted by filmmaker Beat Takeshi, as an art critic. His name has risen to prominence in North America through his last curatorial project, *Superflat*, which brought together nineteen young Japanese artists who collectively represent an accessible art directed at a generation of post-Hirohito youth. As a benevolent manager, he helped these artists gain credibility in Japan by touring the show abroad in the United States.

Murakami's own hyper-commodified work is geared towards young Japanese, many of whom have disposable income to spend in a highly competitive entertainment market. He can be seen as a leader of a new movement of young Japanese artists that has created a crossover of contemporary art into mainstream culture, blurring the line between commercial and fine art. Perhaps the need for that distinction could be considered a Western avant-garde conceit, as Murakami will argue that Hokusai, one of Japan's most celebrated printmakers from the nineteenth century, was in fact working in a highly commercial realm.

The *manga* form itself, as well as evoking a distinct Japanese sensibility, also carries with it a more sinister reference. The quality of *kawaii* (loosely translated as "cuteness") which many characters exude exemplifies an exaggerated or naive happy innocence. In effect, the cuteness of the *manga* image, which developed through the reign of Hirohito, represents a denial of the dominant Japanese social order which should, perhaps, be more willing to observe the emptiness of its own hyper-consumerism.

Further, Murakami has a fascination with *otaku* culture — computer geeks who withdraw from reality through an obsession with fantasy comics. This subculture evokes a darker side of Japan's culture in terms of reflecting a symptomatic sense of depression, a desire to escape into a realm of fantasy far from the realities of Japan's social pressures. With its high-key colouration that sometimes takes on psychedelic overtones, the ear-to-ear grin of Murakami's "Mr. Dob" character adopts an almost menacing and hallucinatory quality. Murakami's Hiropon Factory, then, becomes the metaphoric drug dealer for the *otaku*, the opiate being the fantastic imagery that caters to his users' obsessive and addictive personality type.

In contrast to such an escapist, hyper-commodified strategy of distance, Kaori Yamamoto's photographic series, *Room of Love*, engages intimately with a well-known but little discussed everyday institution, the Love Hotel. Renowned as a site of illicit encounters for businessmen, celebrities and teenage students alike, its kitschy decor and taboo atmosphere make it prime tabloid fodder.

Yamamoto poses herself in these solitary spaces, adopting a variety of iconic female personae such as an OL (office lady), schoolgirl, or prostitute. A kind of fictional history is created in these low budget hotels. (Yamamoto avoids the newer, more upscale Fashion Hotels that cater to fantasy themes, which actually seem ironic of their own bombastic fantasies.) The photographs, as vignettes of imagined trysts, retain a mediated distance through the black and white patina of their "mockumentary" format. As well, the retro-stylings of some of the spaces construct an ambivalent sense of time, a kind of faux-nostalgia that might reference the documentary photography movements of the 1950s and 1960s.

By taking on these disempowered female identities, she gives a face to those women who are usually denied their own presence in the discreet transactions occurring in these hotel rooms. The repetition of Yamamoto's bodily presence as a reenactor of these identities points to her self-reflection and to her criticism of the socially meted roles designated to Japanese women. Upturning the very tenets of these ingrained societal roles, Yamamoto's picturing begins a resistance to Japanese women's enforced passivity and mute identity.

Rika Takahashi's work also dares to make a more directed critical statement regarding a cornerstone of Japanese identity — the icon of the Japanese schoolchild. In opposition to the moral ambivalence of Murakami's *Superflat* artists, who focus on *manga* culture's obsession with the fetishized representation of young schoolgirls as submissive sex objects, Takahashi's work, *Parallel*, addresses the school system itself and its production of an identity of sameness.

Takahashi's installation came out of her concern for children's well-being in the grueling Japanese grade school environment. For twelve years students are subjected to excessive workloads, as they prepare to excel at their final high school exams. This creates a stressful and depressing condition for many children. School also becomes a key site in the formation of Japanese group dynamics, as students are encouraged to work together and resist "standing out" or being too individual.

A line of seven life-size cast forms of young schoolboys march identically upwards on plinths of gradually ascending height. They appear frozen in their social roles; an eerie humanity evoked by the spectrelike figures is obscured by their rote repetition as near-identical forms, literally "molded" as subjects of the state.

The rough hewn texture of these forms (made, incidentally, from recycled milk cartons, revealing an environmental awareness that is finally beginning to enter Japan's consciousness) rejects a commodity glossiness, caught, as they are, between the exactitude of their casting and the coarseness of the pulp material. The work becomes a kind of temporary monument to the struggle of schoolchildren that doesn't resort to grandiose statuesque permanence.

Although Satoru Tamura's animal figurations also work from a representational verisimilitude, his use of the familiar operates towards a different end. Working with a bestiary that includes crocodiles, sharks and, in this installation, bears, Tamura's mechanical animation of these overscaled creatures recalls Japan's pioneering in the field of robotics. In *Standing Bears Go Back*, the animation of his three bear-forms is far from seamless illusion, as they glide down a metal track, the largest with three large openings in its body housing motorized fans.

According to Tamura, his use of animals is, in fact, an arbitrary starting point that is used to generate an autonomous non-referential form. My own narrative bias mistakenly assumed an association with Goldilocks' three bears and then a reference to traditional animism popular to Japanese folklore. The Ainu, for example, still sacrifice a bear, which is said to represent an earthly version of mountain gods. But the strategy of this work is to resist such a literal interpretation and remain referential only to itself, on its objectness in an almost phenomenological manner.

Tamura likens his position to that of a "child's eye" perspective. In one sense this coyness brings to light the assumptions around "reading" a work through a contextual bias. But it is difficult not to dismiss this faux-naive strategy as presumptuous, one that doesn't oblige itself to acknowledge, for example, its aggressive masculine undercurrents.

This last ambivalence brings much to the surface around an ongoing hybrid exchange of ideas that can potentially occur between Japanese and Canadian artists. Importantly, it is an ongoing negotiation between contiguities, not to arrive at a pat solution but to bring forth the unique contexts of the artists and the milieu they come from. The artists from *Kyozon* reveal a great deal about a post-industrial, post-Hirohito Japan, and appear quite at home with a hybrid exchange between East and West. This dialogue need not oblige a literal explanation from artists through their work, but instead provides an awareness of the complexity and constant negotiation involved with cross-cultural exchange.

Thank you to Bertie Mandelblatt, my in-house editor, and Trish Keegan, Kamloops Art Gallery editor, for their careful reading of my text.

A catalogue of the exhibition *Kyozon*, held at the Kamloops Art Gallery
2 December 2001 to 3 February 2002

PRINTED IN CANADA

Published by the Kamloops Art Gallery
101 - 465 Victoria Street,
Kamloops, British Columbia,
Canada V2C 2A9
Telephone: (250) 828-3543
Facsimile: (250) 828-0662
Email: kamloopsartgallery@kag.bc.ca
Website: www.galleries.bc.ca/kamloops

Curator: Susan Edelstein
Editor: Trish Keegan
Photography: Kim Clarke Photography
Design: Steedman Design
Printing: Generation Printing

National Library of Canada Cataloguing in Publication Data
Main entry under title:
Kyozon

  Catalogue of an exhibition held at the Kamloops Art Gallery.
  Includes bibliographical references.
  ISBN 1-895497-49-3

  1. Art, Japanese–21st century—Exhibitions. I. De Forest, Kevin
Ei-ichi, 1962- II. Gagnon, Monika. III. Kimura, Yoichi. IV.
Kamloops Art Gallery.
N7355.K96 2002   709'.52'07471172   C2001-911620-9

The Kamloops Art Gallery is a registered not-for-profit society. We gratefully
acknowledge the financial support of The Canada Council for the Arts, the
Department of Canadian Heritage through the Museums Assistance Program
and Young Canada Works in Heritage Institutions, the Province of British
Columbia through the British Columbia Arts Council and Youth Options BC,
the City of Kamloops, corporate donations and sponsorships, foundation
grants, general donations and memberships.

Kamloops Art Gallery